# from
# Queen
# to
# Empress

# from Queen to Empress

## Victorian Dress 1837–1877

An Exhibition at The Costume Institute
December 15, 1988–April 16, 1989

Caroline Goldthorpe

The Metropolitan Museum of Art
New York
Distributed by Harry N. Abrams, Inc.

This exhibition was made possible by
Laura and John Pomerantz for The Leslie Fay Companies.

Copyright © 1988 by The Metropolitan Museum of Art, New York.

Published by The Metropolitan Museum of Art
and distributed to the trade by Harry N. Abrams, Inc.,
100 Fifth Avenue, New York, NY 10011.

John P. O'Neill, Editor in Chief
Barbara Burn, Executive Editor and Project Supervisor
Michael Shroyer, Designer

All photographs in this book not otherwise credited
were taken by Sheldan Comfort Collins.

All costumes in this book, unless otherwise noted,
are in the collection of The Costume Institute,
The Metropolitan Museum of Art.

Library of Congress Cataloging-in-Publication Data

Goldthorpe, Caroline.
    From Queen to Empress: Victorian dress 1837-1877: an exhibition at
  the Costume Institute, December 15, 1988-April 16, 1989/Caroline
  Goldthorpe.
      p. cm.
    Bibliography: p.
    ISBN 0-87099-534-0. ISBN 0-87099-535-9 (pbk.). ISBN
  0-8109-1178-7 (Abrams)
    1. Costume—Great Britain—History—19th century—Exhibitions.
  2. Costume—History—19th century—Exhibitions. 3. Costume Institute
  (New York, N.Y.)—Exhibitions. I. Costume Institute (New York, N.Y.)
  II. Title.
  GT737.G65 1988
  390'.00941'07401—dc19                                         88-39952
                                                                    CIP

Typeset by Office Services, The Metropolitan Museum of Art
Printed by Meridian Printing, Rhode Island
Bound by Publishers Book Bindery, Inc., Long Island City, New York

*Cover/Jacket: Portrait Group of Queen Victoria with the Children*
by John Callcott Horsley (The FORBES Magazine Collection, New York).

ISBN: 0-87099-534-0
ISBN: 0-87099-535-9 (pbk)
ISBN: 0-8109-1178-7 (H. N. Abrams)

# Contents

# Director's Foreword

For the English-speaking world, most of the nineteenth century is thought of as the Victorian era, when the visual arts, music, and literature—as well as the manners and qualities of mind they represented—were imbued with the aura of the Queen of England. The latter part of the reign, the luxurious and audacious Belle Epoque, is by far the most familiar to us now, but this period was firmly rooted in the turmoil of the four preceding decades, when the rapid expansion of industrialized society brought the glories of the machine age face to face with the misery of social ills and unrest. Art criticism reflected the tumultuous nature of the time. The nearly limitless possibilities of machine-made objects inspired numerous romantic revivals in style and ornamentation. The combination of Gothic architectural elements to form the base of a lamp, for example, was invariably condemned by critics bent on reforming romantic fantasies into designs with a greater unity of style and purpose. The efforts of these critics culminated in the Great Exhibition of 1851, which demonstrated a new mood of national optimism and solidified the popularity of Victoria and Albert. Industrial prosperity had brought about increased personal income as well as profits, and all sectors of society benefited. The Great Exhibition provided the critics with a spectacular forum in which to test their theories, and it gave Sir Joseph Paxton the opportunity to design the Crystal Palace, an edifice of glass and iron that became a landmark in the development of modern architecture. Rising confidence reconfirmed the importance of standards of excellence—codes of behavior in private life; codes of taste in the arts—and the royal family came to represent the high moral standard for domestic life throughout the Empire.

The costumes in this exhibition, drawn primarily from the Costume Institute's collection, embody many of the complex aspects of mid-nineteenth-century English design. The textiles, which include rich silks as well as printed cottons, demonstrate the mastery of mechanical techniques for weaving and printing and serve as examples from both sides of the critical argument about the appropriateness of illusionism and the relationship between design and function. These fashionable silhouettes and their decorative trimmings reflect the period's taste for romantic revivals. There is also evidence of the sentimentality that supported the strict standards of behavior for women—chastity, modesty, and a sense of duty.

The study of costumes as art-historical documents illustrating important aesthetic ideas and theories is a guiding principle of the acquisition and exhibition policies of The Costume Institute. This display of early- to mid-Victorian fashion is a valuable contribution to that study, and I would like to thank the Costume Institute staff for their considerable efforts, especially curatorial assistant Caroline Goldthorpe, who selected the costumes, supervised their display and photography, and provided the text for this book. A generous grant from Laura and John Pomerantz for the Leslie Fay Companies has made the exhibition possible, and I wish to express my sincere appreciation for their gift.

Philippe de Montebello
Director

Our family and The Leslie Fay Companies
have been supporters of The Costume Institute
for more than thirty years,
and it gives us great pleasure to be the sponsor
of the exhibition
*From Queen to Empress: Victorian Dress 1837–1877.*

This fascinating exhibition documents
the life and the fashions of one of the most
interesting periods of the last century.

Laura and John Pomerantz
for The Leslie Fay Companies, Inc.

B. London May 15th 1838. My original study
of the Queen of England. Victoria 1st
Painted from life.
Buckingham House

# Introduction

Fashion is a necessity of human nature; because while we all desire to be pleasingly attired, not one in 10,000 of us is able to invent any article of dress or decoration that shall be truly becoming. . . . We are so constituted that we like to be like one another; and so general is this desire, that one of the signs of madness is an inclination to oddity in personal adornment. It is hard for us to believe in the soundness of a person's judgement who turns his collar down when everyone else turns it up, or who lets his hair grow very long when the rest of mankind have theirs cropped. Indeed, there are circles, even in metropolitan London, Paris or New York, where a person otherwise unexceptionable, would be grossly undervalued if he should present himself in any other than the regulation coat.

*The Atlantic Monthly,* 1869

During the nineteenth century both England and America looked to France for the latest developments and innovations in fashion, and fashionable dress was clearly international in the Victorian era, as observed by *The Atlantic Monthly* writer quoted above, although French styles were often diluted and adapted abroad. Noting that the right coat was required for the right occasion, the author implies that the same coat would do for London and New York as well as Paris.

The first forty years of Victoria's reign were particularly rich in costume history in both England and America. The simple silhouette and printed cottons of the early nineteenth century gave way to luxurious silks and an extraordinary diversity of costume shapes. This was a time for considerable innovation, with the invention of the sewing machine in the 1840s and the introduction of the first aniline, or synthetic, dyes, which produced stronger, brighter hues than had formerly been possible. Advances of the machine age that were used in dressmaking enabled huge, domed skirts to be supported by wafer-thin circles of steel and corsets to be steam-molded into particular shapes.

*Opposite: Queen Victoria* by Thomas Sully (1783–1872), 1838. This oil sketch was painted from life during several sittings in the spring of 1838, just before the coronation, in preparation for a full-length portrait. Victoria, who wears a diamond diadem, earrings, and necklace, is said to have considered this "a nice picture." (Bequest of T. S. Darley, 1914, 14.126.1)

To a greater or lesser extent, fashion influenced the dress of all except the very poorest sections of society, but those who had the money and leisure to follow fashion most closely were the upper and upper-middle classes, at a time when class structure was still rigidly observed. Consider the fact that a lavish trousseau was advertised for £100 in 1867, while a survey made in the same year indicated that nearly 88 percent of the English population earned less than £100 a year.

The upper levels of society in Britain, Europe, and America were as international as their fashions, since the long-established aristocratic families tended to mix socially and to intermarry. The aspiring middle classes closely followed the minutiae of aristocratic behavior. To ensure that every detail of life was conducted properly and to enable them to avoid the numerous social pitfalls, an increasing number of ladies' magazines spelled out correct etiquette for each and every occasion. The editors of these magazines set the standard that dominated the lives of respectable housewives by producing pages full of information, including the niceties of proper dress, fabrics, and accessories. These magazines were all generously illustrated with fashion plates, often hand-colored, showing the Parisian style of the moment, albeit in an idealized form. As the same plates were used throughout Europe, Britain, and America, every new fashion was disseminated speedily and enabled provincial costume to keep up with the capitals.

Queen Victoria, who came to the throne in 1837 at the age of eighteen and ruled until 1901, has come to personify the greater part of the nineteenth century, and the term "Victorian" has been applied to the era in both England and America. The route by which Victoria became Queen was a tortuous one, beginning in 1817 with the death of the only child of the future George IV. The direct line to the throne had thus ended, and the crown would pass on George's death to his brother, William IV, whose children had died as infants. Next in line to William was the Duke of Kent, Victoria's father, but he died shortly after Victoria was born, on May 24, 1819. Victoria knew, then, from a very young age that she was to become Queen.

The apparent fragility of the monarchical line may in part explain why Victoria and Albert produced as many as nine children, although she disliked being pregnant and disapproved of those who were too often pregnant: "It is more like a rabbit or guinea-pig than anything else and really it is not very nice."

By the time Victoria was declared Empress at the celebrations in India in January 1877, the English royal family was firmly established. Through a network of carefully chosen marriages for her children, Victoria was now linked with some of the most powerful royal families on the continent, including Germany and Russia.

# from Queen to Empress

# Royal Influence

Since Victoria had been brought up from birth to be Queen of England, she was well aware of the significance of her example in all things, including dress. For all important public appearances, therefore, she invariably wore costumes of British manufacture. In 1838 her coronation robes had been specially woven in the Spitalfields silk-weaving area of London, as was her cream-colored satin wedding dress in 1840. The lace for her wedding, despite rumors in the press that it would be the more fashionable "Brussels point," was actually handmade Honiton lace, worn in a deliberate attempt to assist a declining industry through royal patronage. As a result, immediately following the wedding, at least one London lace retailer switched the emphasis of his advertisements to concentrate on Honiton lace.

Queen Victoria commissioned a portrait of herself from Franz Xaver Winterhalter (figure 1), for which she sat in June and July of 1842. The painting shows a deep flounce of lace covering the lower section of the satin skirt, with a bertha at the neck, very much like the arrangement on her wedding gown. The portrait was completed in August and set into the wall of the White Drawing Room at Windsor Castle. Winterhalter was immediately commissioned to paint at least three copies, and a number of others exist, including enamel miniatures that the Queen had made up into bracelets for her friends.

For the state entry of Queen Victoria and Prince Albert into Paris in 1855, the Queen wore a dress of white Spitalfields silk, its design representing an English flower garden (figure 2). While in Paris, however, she attended a ball at the Hôtel de Ville, wearing "my diamond diadem with the Koh-i-noor in it, a white net dress, embroidered with gold and (as were all my dresses) very full. It was very much admired by the Emperor and the ladies. The Emperor asked if it was English; I said No, it had been made on purpose in Paris." In addition

1. *Queen Victoria* by Franz Xaver Winterhalter (1805–1873), after an original painting by the artist for which the Queen sat in June and July 1842. The Queen wears a dress of heavy ivory satin, enhanced by a bertha and a deep flounce of lace like those on her wedding dress (see figure 39). Her jewelry includes a diadem of sapphires and diamonds, the huge sapphire-and-diamond brooch given to her by Prince Albert on their wedding day, and the Order of the Garter insignia. (The FORBES Magazine Collection, New York)

to the ball gown, made in France as a diplomatic gesture, she evidently wore both English and French silks for less public occasions. Two days later she wrote in her diary again: "Rested, but had to choose quantities of Lyons silk &c, while I was lying on the nice sofa."

During her reign Victoria actively fueled the increasing popular interest in historic dress by holding three fancy-dress balls. The first, held in 1842, was set in fourteenth-century England, with Victoria and Albert dressed as Queen Philippa and King Edward III. *The Illustrated London News* described the ball as "a magnificent scene of historic revelry" and welcomed the extravagance: "The purpose of this splendid gathering of the brave and beautiful, it is known, was to give stimulus to trade in all the various departments that could be affected by the enormous outlay it would necessarily involve, and we have no doubt that many thousands are this day grateful for the temporary aid which this right royal entertainment has been the means of affording them."

The second costume ball, held in 1845, had a mid-eighteenth-century theme, and the ball in 1851 had as a setting the court of Charles II, at which the American Minister appeared in the costume of John Winthrop, Governor of the New England colonies from 1657 to 1676. Vast sums were clearly spent not only on the balls themselves but also on all the costumes, estimated to have cost up to £800 each and designed to achieve a high degree of historical accuracy.

The importance of visible royal patronage was not lost on commercial enterprise, and in 1863 the Norwich shawl manufacturers Clabburn Sons & Crisp sent to Princess Alexandra of Denmark, as a gift on the occasion of her marriage to the Prince of Wales, a magnificent silk shawl woven in the Danish royal colors (figure 3). The Queen herself already patronized Norwich shawls, for in 1849 the *Journal of Design* had claimed: "The shawls of Norwich now equal the richest production of the looms of France. The success which attended the exhibition of Norwich shawls . . . may fairly be considered the result of Her Majesty's direct regard." Another splendid silk shawl by Clabburn Sons & Crisp was displayed at the International Exhibition of 1862 (figure 4), but it was not eligible for a prize because William Clabburn himself was on the panel of judges.

The first international exhibition ever held was the Great Exhibition of the Works of Industry of all Nations in 1851, which had been masterminded by Prince Albert, who saw it as much more than a trade fair: "The Exhibition of 1851 is to give us a true test and a living picture of the point of development at which the whole of mankind has arrived . . . and a new starting point from which all nations will be able to direct their further exertions." The exhibition building, designed by Joseph Paxton and dubbed "The Crystal Palace"

2. English-made dress of Spitalfields silk. This dress was worn by Queen Victoria for her state entry into Paris in August 1855. The elaborate warp-printed design depicts an English flower garden. (Museum of London)

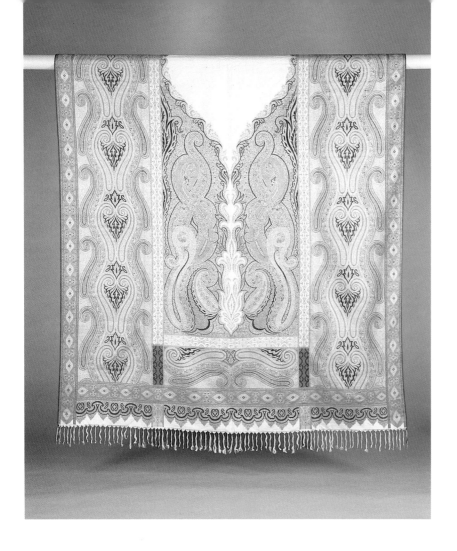

3. Detail of an English silk shawl woven in the Danish royal colors, a prototype for the shawl presented to Princess Alexandra of Denmark on the occasion of her marriage to the Prince of Wales on March 10, 1863. (Norfolk Museums Service)

4. Detail of another silk shawl woven by Clabburn Sons & Crisp, displayed at the 1862 International Exhibition in London. The shawl's enormous size, approximately six by twelve feet, is typical of the 1850s and 1860s. (Norfolk Museums Service)

5. English dress of pink silk, woven with silver motifs, worn by Queen Victoria for the ceremony opening the Great Exhibition, May 1, 1851. (Museum of London)

by *Punch*, covered nineteen acres of Hyde Park. One hundred thousand objects shown by 17,000 exhibitors from all over the globe were seen by more than six million visitors between May 1 and October.

Queen Victoria opened the exhibition, accompanied by Prince Albert and their two oldest children—the Princess Royal, aged ten, and the Prince of Wales, aged nine. The Queen recorded the event in her diary as a triumph: "This day is one of the greatest and most glorious days of our lives. At ½ past 11 the whole procession in 9 State carriages was set in motion. Vicky and Bertie were in our carriage. . . . Vicky was dressed in lace over white satin, with a small wreath of pink silk roses in her hair, and looked very nice. Bertie was in full highland dress. . . . I forgot to mention that I wore a dress of pink and silver, with a diamond ray diadem and little crown at the back with 2 feathers, all the rest of my jewels being diamonds." This dress, made of pink silk figured with interlinked silver circles and trimmed with pink bows, is now in the collection of the Museum of London (figure 5).

In 1854 the Crystal Palace was re-created in a modified form at Sydenham, just outside London, and was once again opened by the Queen. The rather idealized portrait group reproduced here (figure 6) was painted by John Callcott Horsley of the Queen and seven of her nine children and is probably meant to be set in about 1854. The Crystal Palace can be seen both in the background and in the original drawing held by the Prince of Wales. The painting is an invaluable study of fashionable children's clothing at a time when children were dressed as miniature versions of their parents (the little girls even wore tiny crinolines and bustles) and when the dress of the royal children was particularly influential. The Queen particularly liked the Highland outfit for her sons, and on many ceremonial occasions the Prince of Wales was dressed as he is here. The tiny sailor suit made for him to wear on the royal yacht in the summer of 1846 set a trend, reinforced by his own children, that was to last well into the twentieth century.

The huge success of the Great Exhibition encouraged innumerable others—Cork in 1852, Dublin and New York in 1853, Munich in 1854, and Paris in 1855. In 1862 a second international exhibition was held in London, followed by another in Paris in 1867.

There were relatively few complete costumes displayed in the international exhibitions, but accessories and fabrics were featured, and a curious number of elements were subsequently extracted from their original context and grafted onto fashionable dress. *The Englishwoman's Domestic Magazine* in 1867 reported: "This year's fashions seem to borrow something from the number of foreign costumes that are seen in Paris since the opening of the Great Exhibition. Amongst these the most eccentric are those that meet the most favour. Thus we have Chinese sleeves, Egyptian girdles, Turkish jackets. . . . It becomes more difficult than ever to dress really well and in good taste, and to avoid these fashions which are too much exaggerated to be ladylike."

The most obvious aspect of costume in which the example of Queen Victoria was extremely influential was that of mourning dress. She had always observed correct mourning etiquette, but after December 14, 1861, when her beloved Albert died suddenly, she was completely bereft and withdrew utterly from the public gaze. When she did emerge from her isolation, she no longer followed current fashions in dress but wore black for the rest of her life, becoming the archetypal widow and fanning the cult of mourning through the second half of the nineteenth century.

# Underdress

Throughout the period from 1837 to 1877, the silhouette sought by the lady of fashion was an artificial one, created by various undergarments designed to give additional volume to one area or to reduce undesirable fullness in another. In order to understand how the variety of shapes adopted by the Victorian lady was achieved, it is necessary to look first at the basic structures or foundations over which the fashionable styles of the period were arranged.

The ideal shape of the late 1830s was a long, slim torso, emphasized by the dropped waist of the dress. To ensure this shape, a corset (or stays) extended "not only over the bosom, but also all over the abdomen and back down to the hips" (*Handbook of the Toilet*). Newly introduced metal eyelets enabled ladies to have their corsets laced more tightly, even though they complained that as a result "they cannot sit upright without them," as one writer remarked in 1837. "The proper object of 'The Complete Corset' should evidently be gently to support the figure, without diminishing the freedom of motion and to conceal the size of the abdomen when it becomes disproportionately large, either from corpulence, or from accidents which naturally occur" (pregnancy). Next to the skin under the corset the lady wore a half-length linen chemise, which was visible above and below the corset but cut sufficiently low that it did not show when the lady was dressed. Lengths of whalebone were stitched into gussets to give the corset the required shape; it was laced up the back and a full-skirted petticoat was worn over it. Stockings at this date were of knitted silk, usually white, held up with loosely tied garters.

The slender, corseted waist was accompanied by a skirt that steadily grew in volume throughout the century. As early as 1839 *Townsend's Parisian Fashions* noted that "horse-hair under-petticoats are now almost universally adopted." These stiff underskirts were placed "underneath the Cambric petticoat, and serve to give that fullness to the dress, which is now so fashionable as to be indispensable." The number and volume

**7.** *A Young Woman at Her Dressing Table* by Augustus Egg (1816–1863), c. 1850. The lady, who is dressing for the evening, wears a taffeta underskirt, a linen or cotton chemise edged with lace, and a heavy, shaped corset. (Collection of Edmund J. and Suzanne McCormick)

of petticoats continued to increase, and some underskirts were enlarged and stiffened by rows of inserted cording. The outermost petticoats were always elaborately embroidered or trimmed with crochet and lace. Where the petticoat did not have a bodice, a camisole was worn over the corset to protect the dress.

Another protective garment that became popular at the time were drawers, which reached below the knee and were cut very full but left open all along the inside seam and secured only at the bottom of each leg. In 1841 the *Handbook of the Toilet* recommended drawers to an uncertain audience: "In France, drawers form a necessary part of female attire and many indispositions, to which our British females are continually subject, are prevented by their use. According to our fastidious notions of propriety it is considered indelicate to allude in any way to the limbs of ladies, yet I am obliged to break the ice of this foolish etiquette."

By the late 1840s, as the waist of the dress began to rise to meet that of the wearer, it was deemed necessary for the waist itself to be as small as possible, and so a new type of short corset, made from numerous shaped sections, was developed. To ensure a fashionably slender adult figure, girls were often put into corsets at an early age. By this time fashionable stockings were made of cotton as well as silk and were held up with garters of elastic fastened by metal clasps.

In April 1855 the *Petit Courier des Dames* advised: "In order to attain the enormous circumference which the exaggerated 'rondeur' of the dresses demand today, petticoats of crinoline [horse-hair] are not enough, some instead are made in pique with five rows of very thin, supple whalebone, from the hem up to the knees. These petticoats give perfect support, but are a little too stiff and bell-like. That is why the elegant woman always prefers petticoats . . . with three fluted flounces." In addition to the requisite stiffly starched under-petticoats, quilted examples were introduced for warmth in the winter. Not only did all these petticoats impede physical movement, but as they were so long and heavy they were criticized for being dirty and harmful to the health. "More ladies catch colds from wet skirts flapping against the ankle, than even from wet feet," claimed *Peterson's Magazine*.

August Egg's painting *A Young Woman at Her Dressing Table* (figure 7), which shows a fashionable belle of the 1850s changing into evening dress, is one of the rare depictions of Victorian underwear. The shaped front of the strapless corset and the lace-trimmed chemise can be clearly seen. The skirt of the dress, with lavish flounces of black lace, and a headdress of fresh flowers are visible at the lady's side.

The artificial cage crinoline was introduced in 1856. Made from thin strips of metal suspended by tapes one from another in ever-widening circles, this structure could support the full

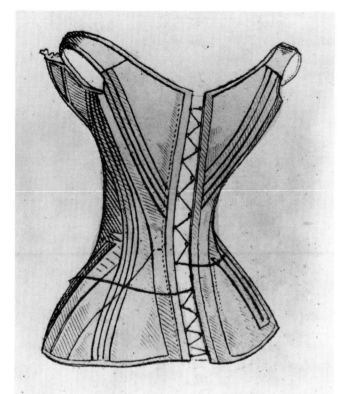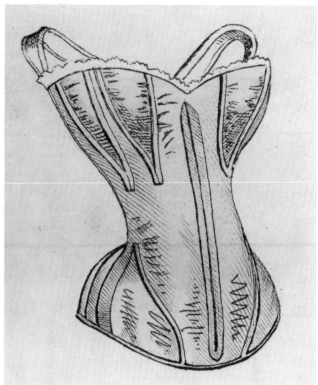

width of the skirt by itself, and it gave the wearer far more freedom of movement than she had had under the weight and bulk of many petticoats. Nevertheless, its diameter of up to four feet presented difficulties for those around her.

Because of the risk that a high wind might reveal a glimpse of leg, it became common for ladies to wear full-length pantaloons edged with lace, a style originally worn by small girls. The *Petit Courier des Dames* bemoaned the fact that "one cannot hope for much modification in the volume of skirts, for the main occupation at the moment is inventing systems whereby the enormous circumference of deep pleats can be supported," and, indeed, armed with the improved technology, the skirts were now able to grow still larger.

Accompanying the fashion for the huge skirt was that of the tiny waist, for the two were intended to complement each other. One correspondent to the *Englishwoman's Domestic Magazine* in 1867 spoke out in defense of tight lacing, which was being increasingly criticized by the medical profession: "I was placed, at the age of fifteen, at a fashionable school in London, and there it was the custom for the waists of the pupils to be reduced one inch per month. When I left school at seventeen my waist measured only thirteen inches, it having been formerly twenty three inches. Every morning, one of the maids used to come to assist us to dress . . . to see that our corsets were drawn as tightly as possible. After the first few minutes every morning, I felt no pain, and the only ill effects, apparently, were occasional headaches and loss of appetite."

8, 9. Two details from a fashion plate in *Tages Bericht* (c. 1840), showing the front and back of a corset. The long corset, which was laced up the back, was made up of shaped sections, with strips of whalebone stitched in, which forced the body into the shape required by the fashion of the day.

From 1860 on the circular shape of the crinoline began to alter, becoming flatter at the front and larger at the back, as reported in the *Englishwoman's Domestic Magazine* in 1862: "Crinolines are very much reduced in size at the top, but retain their amplitude at the bottom and are made with trains to suit the fashionable skirts."

As with most new styles the crinoline, initially worn only by fashionable high society, was soon adopted by aspiring women of other social classes. In England the Staffordshire Potteries forbade the wearing of crinolines by their workwomen after more than £200 worth of articles had been broken by them in one year. Courtauld's Mills issued a similar warning: "The present ugly fashion of hoops or Crinoline, as it is called, is quite unfitted for the work of our factories. . . . It is highly dangerous . . . greatly impedes free passage . . . and sometimes becomes shockingly indecent."

Even with the privations suffered by the American South during the blockades of the Civil War, a Mrs. McGuire recounted in her diary: "A lady in Richmond said laughingly to a friend who was about to make an effort to go to Baltimore 'Bring me a pound of tea and a hoop-skirt,' and after a very short absence he appeared before her, with the tea in one hand and the skirt in the other."

Fashion eventually dictated that the long trailing skirts were to be gathered up at the back, and an extra horsehair flounce was added at the back of the waist, between the skirt and the crinoline. In 1866 and 1867 other alternatives to the crinoline were reported as being favored by the fashionable world, and in 1868 the crinoline shrank drastically to a modest cone foundation. The supporting flounce now took over the role of determining the silhouette, in the form of a bustle, or tournure. There was an increasing use of colored underwear during the day in the 1860s, particularly of scarlet petticoats worn with colored stockings of wool, cotton, or silk.

As the skirt became even narrower, the *Milliner and Dressmaker* of 1873 recommended that "no crinoline of any kind is worn excepting the Tournure of fine white horsehair to keep up the puff in the upper part of the dress. The best model is that which is formed of a number of flutings . . . as it keeps up better than anything." Slowly the tournure began to slip down and become longer, extending down the back of the skirt to the knee and worn with an elongated, flounced petticoat to support the newly fashionable train. Following the style of dress, underclothing became increasingly elaborate, with a profusion of trimming. Drawers were still optional and four possible styles of chemise existed until 1877, when the "combination" was invented to merge drawers and chemise in one garment.

Since the dress was now virtually molded to fit the figure, the correct shape of the corset was essential. The following

advertisement was reprinted in *Punch* in 1877: "Buy a pair of Maintenon corsets, fitting your waist measure. The other parts of the corset will be proportioned as you ought to be. Put the corset on, and fill in the vacant spaces with fine jeweller's wool, then tack on a piece of soft silk or cambric over the bust thus formed to keep the wool in place, renewing it as often as required."

One form of clothing that falls between dress and undress is the wrapper. Perhaps closest to a modern-day housecoat, it was also called a peignoir, although that term referred as well to other types of clothing. The fullness of the wrapper's skirt and the shape of its sleeve followed the general line of fashionable day dress, but it was a looser, less formal garment, which fastened down the front over an embroidered or lace-trimmed underdress or underskirt. Two wrappers in the Costume Institute collection that date from the mid-1850s (figure 12) are typical in their use of strong, contrasting colors and in their fashionable pagoda sleeves. They are both constructed with heavy pleating of the skirt material to the waistband at the back, but with a less constricting cut in front. The wrappers fasten with a double row of buttons secured by silk loops and a silk cord belt.

**11.** Plate from *Frank Leslie's Monthly Magazine*, May 1863, illustrating a cage crinoline of the early 1860s. The crinoline is described in the magazine as "gradually widening to four yards at the bottom, where it is covered with horsehair, terminating in a flounce of the same material."

In 1847 Elizabeth Bancroft, wife of the American Minister to England, wrote home from a weekend party: "Let me tell Aunty that our simple breakfast dress is unknown in England. You come down in the morning dressed for the day until six or seven in the evening." In fact, wrappers were popular in England, but on house-party weekends, correct etiquette probably required more formal wear.

Although the wrapper was an informal garment, when the corset might perhaps not be laced so tightly, it was by no means casual. It had a distinct place in the strict regimen of appropriate dress and was still governed by the requirements and restrictions of propriety, as *The Ladies Book of Etiquette*, published in the late 1870s, made abundantly clear: "The most suitable dress for breakfast is a wrapper, made to fit the figure loosely. It is much better to let the hair be perfectly smooth, requiring no cap, which is often worn to conceal the lazy slovenly arrangement of the hair. . . . Slippers of embroidered cloth are prettiest with a wrapper. . . . A lady should never receive her morning callers in a wrapper, unless they call at an unusually early hour, or some unexpected demand upon her time makes it impossible to change her dress after breakfast. . . . Let each dress worn by a lady be suitable to the occasion upon which she wears it. A toilet may be as offensive to good taste and propriety by being too elaborate, as by being slovenly. . . . It is in as bad taste to receive your morning calls in an elaborate evening dress, as it would be to attend a ball in your morning wrapper."

**12.** Two silk wrappers that fasten down the front with elaborate loop-and-button closures and a silk cord belt. American, mid-1850s. (Left: Gift of Mrs. Edwin R. Metcalf, 1969, CI 69.32.5; right: Gift of The New-York Historical Society, 1979, 1979.346.19)

# Day Dress

A t the time Queen Victoria came to the throne in 1837, a particular silhouette was in the process of evolving. The skirt had been widening at the hem since the decline of the columnar Neoclassical lines of the early nineteenth century, while the natural waist had returned. During the early 1830s the sleeve grew to vast dimensions beneath a variety of flamboyant hats and hairstyles.

In 1836 an alternative to the great volume of the sleeve was introduced, as reported in *The Poetry of Travelling in the United States*. "Almost the first small sleeves that have been seen in America for seven years [appeared in Washington] on the person of a Virginia lady who had been to France. What a sensation! There was half a shudder among the company as they felt the immense sacks on their arms, contrasted with those new sleeves without any relieving plait, tight—tight as a suit of armor, from the shoulder to the elbow." Fashion, however, was merely offering this smaller sleeve as a variation; as the fullness of the sleeve began to shrink and move down the arm, its material was gathered at the shoulder, kept full below and then tight along the lower arm.

To contrast with the narrow waist, the width of the low, straight neckline was emphasized, and soft folds of material were often added near the top of the bodice, caught in the center by a narrow band. Two examples in the Costume Institute collection illustrate this treatment of the bodice and sleeves (figure 13 left, figure 14 right). It is interesting that one of these dresses is a printed cotton and one is a silk satin; silks were increasingly worn at this period for day dress. Another method for giving extra width to the shoulders was the use of a pelerine, a short cape made of muslin or of the dress material itself.

The bodice and skirt were usually made as a one-piece dress, fastened in back by means of hooks and eyes. By 1840 the bodice had become elongated, with a low, pointed waist

13. Left: American satin day dress, c. 1837. The volume of the sleeve is gathered in at the shoulder and the top of the bodice is decorated with a horizontal trim. (Gift of Louise Dahl-Wolfe, 1949, CI 49.44) Right: English satin day dress, c. 1842. The fitted sleeves and the ruching and trim in the same fabric emphasize the elongated bodice and low, pointed waist. (Purchase, Irene Lewisohn Trust, Gift, 1986, 1986.106.2)

**14.** Left: American day dress, c. 1840, of white cotton printed with vertical figured stripes and diagonal bands of color. The mancherons, or upper sleeves, are unusually long and narrow. (Gift of George Wells, 1978, 1978.392.1) Right: American day dress of cream cotton, c. 1837. The multicolored floral print is worn with a finely embroidered pelerine. The treatment of the bodice trim and upper sleeve matches the satin example in figure 13. (Gift of Claggett Wilson, 1938, 38.53)

**15.** English day dress of silk and wool, c. 1844. An increasing naturalism has replaced the heavily stylized prints of the 1830s. (Purchase, Marcia Sand Bequest, in memory of her daughter, Tiger [Joan] Morse, 1979, 1979.385.2)

accentuated by decoration on the dress (figure 13 right). The sleeves were either made very tight with the addition of a short upper sleeve, or mancheron (figure 14 left), or some fullness was retained at the elbow. The sleeves were set into the bodice at a much lower level, which thereby restricted the movements of the arm.

As the skirt continued to grow in width, a new method of attaching it to the bodice was devised, using very tight organ pleats secured at every other fold. This allowed the bodice to retain the narrow waist in spite of the extra fullness and greatly increased the volume of the skirt, causing it to spring out from the waist in a domelike shape.

To emphasize the bodice, extra fullness of material was gathered into a blunt point at the waist, creating fan-shaped folds up to the neckline. A subsequent variation on this theme added a false front of extra material gathered at the shoulders and waist. The tightness of the sleeve began to soften from

VASEY.

16. Two silk day dresses, English (left) and American (right), c. 1850. Additional material on the bodice front has been gathered to a blunt point; the wide pagoda sleeves are trimmed with fringing typical of the period. (Right: Purchase, Mr. and Mrs. Alan S. Davis, Gift, 1981, 1981.14.1ab; left: Purchase, Irene Lewisohn Trust, Gift, 1986, 1986.106.9ab)

17. Plate from *The Family Herald*, showing Mrs. Amelia Bloomer wearing "the new costume," as she had appeared in her own periodical, *The Lily*.

the mid-1840s on, becoming slightly wider at the wrist. As the hem dropped from ankle length to floor length, it became usual for skirts to be edged with a narrow "brush-braid," which protruded just below the bottom of the skirt. This edging protected the material from dirt and wear and could be easily removed and replaced.

Fashionable footwear of the 1840s was essentially a flat slipper, disparaged by *The Ladies' Repository* in 1843: "Amidst the frosts of winter, and the damp of spring the devotee of fashion may be seen walking the streets with no more substantial covering for her feet than the silken hose and the Parisian sole—affording scarce greater protection than the stocking itself and this notwithstanding the many instances in which such exposure annually results in early death or a broken constitution."

**18.** American day dress of silk and wool, early 1850s. This dress is woven with a fine silk check pattern and richly printed in a multi-colored design, with three flounces *à disposition*, edged with a multi-colored silk fringe. (Gift of Claire Lorraine Wilson, 1941, CI 42.76.3)

**19.** *Doubtful Fortune* by Abraham
Solomon (1824–1862), shown at
the Royal Academy, London, in
1856. The three ladies wear typical
day dresses of the mid-1850s; note
the similarity between the young
lady in pink and the dress in figure
20. (Collection of Edmund J. and
Suzanne McCormick)

**20.** English day dress of striped silk, c. 1854–56. The elongated jacket bodice flares out over the skirt, which is widened by three stiff flounces woven *à disposition*. (Purchase, Irene Lewisohn Bequest, 1987, 1987.190.2ab)

**21.** Photograph of Queen Victoria and Prince Albert taken by J. J. E. Mayall on March 1, 1861. Beneath her dress, the Queen is wearing a round crinoline, its width accentuated by the two deep flounces with horizontal stripes. (Copyright reserved. Reproduced by gracious permission of Her Majesty Queen Elizabeth II)

Fashion continued to dictate an increasingly wide skirt during the 1840s. *The Handbook of Dressmaking* in 1847 recommended a French technique for achieving the desired effect: "Crinoline, or woven horse-hair, is introduced in wide strips into the hem of the skirt; should it be wished to make the skirt appear very full, two pieces of the crinoline may be laid on in bands up the skirt enclosed in lining muslin." Echoing the shape of the skirt, the sleeve too began to expand, opening from the elbow into a funnel shape, which required the wearing of undersleeves to cover the lower arms. The skirt could now be separate from the new jacket-style bodice, which was worn either closed or open over a visible, decorated chemisette, or underblouse.

At this point, in reaction to the volume of the skirt and the weight and heat of the petticoats required to support it, a slightly revised form of dress appeared, first worn by an American, one Mrs. Miller, who had seen it in a ladies' health sanitarium in Switzerland (figure 17). Mrs. Miller was a friend of Amelia Bloomer, a leader of the women's rights movement, and she promoted the new garment in her monthly newspaper,

*The Lily*, in February 1851: "We would have the skirt reaching down to nearly halfway between the knee and the ankle, and not made quite so full as is the present fashion. Underneath this skirt, trousers made moderately full, in fair mild weather coming down to the ankle (not instep) and there gathered in with an elastic band. The shoes or slippers to suit the occasion. For winter or wet weather, the trousers also full, but coming down into a boot."

This apparently minor and sensible alteration of contemporary dress, however, by its association with the women's movement, was greeted with outrage and ridicule in the press. Throughout 1851 the so-called "Bloomer costume" made a brave effort to infiltrate the fashionable world. *The Family Herald* reported a number of women in the major cities of England wearing it "but unnerved by the persecuting curiosity excited by the transatlantic garb." It was reported to have gone out of fashion by April 1852.

Although it made such a brief appearance, the Bloomer costume is of interest as the forerunner of a number of outfits intended for sporting activities, particularly the bathing costume of the mid-1860s. Moreover, Mrs. Merrifield in *Dress as a Fine Art* recognized that "had the Bloomer costume . . . been introduced by a tall and graceful scion of the aristocracy, either of rank or talent, instead of being first adopted by the middle ranks, it might have met with better success. . . . We are content to adopt the greatest absurdities in dress when they are brought from Paris, or recommended by a French name, but American fashions have no chance of success in aristocratic England, it is beginning at the wrong end."

Meanwhile, high fashion of the 1850s saw a change in the construction of the skirt to cope with the ever-increasing volume of material. This involved the use of pleats at the side with gathers only at the back. Bodices were increasingly fastened in front, which led to a fashion for using more ornamental buttons; the new, detachable button was held in place by a split pin so that a complete set could be easily replaced. The watch-pocket, which had appeared hidden in the folds of the dress in the 1840s, now moved to the waist seam, and the large inside pocket opened from one of the skirt seams.

There was a movement away from the quieter, more harmonious tones of the 1840s toward a greater use of bright, contrasting colors. Tartans were much used, but one writer advised in 1850 that "check materials are not worn by the ladies, being entirely given up to the nether integuments of the sterner sex."

Flounces on the skirt, which had begun to appear in the 1840s, were indispensable by 1853 to add necessary fullness to the width of a skirt. This width was accentuated by the jacket bodice, which extended over the hips. There was a great

22. English satin day bodice and skirt, trimmed with velvet ribbon, c. 1865. Figure 35 shows an evening bodice designed to be worn with the same skirt. Suspended from the waist is a cut-steel chatelaine, with a tiny almanac for 1866, a thimble-holder, a needle and pin case, a pencil, and a memo tablet with ivory pages. (Gift of Irene Lewisohn, 1937, 37.46.37a,c)

fashion for flounces "*à disposition*," in which the material to be used for the flounces was woven or printed specifically, matching but distinct from the rest of the dress (figure 18). Fringe trimming on the bodice was increasingly popular, and the very full, open pagoda sleeves had become the most common form, often slit at the front. The painting *Doubtful Fortune* by Abraham Solomon (figure 19), shown at the Royal Academy in 1856, provides an excellent depiction of the day dress of the time. Note especially the figure in pink whose full skirt is enlarged by three flounces and emphasized by the cut of her elongated jacket bodice. The bodice itself is edged with fringing and a lace collar at the neck, and the full sleeve opens over a lace undersleeve. This dress is similar to the black and teal blue corded silk example in the Costume Institute collection (figure 20), although there the horizontal stripes serve to add further emphasis to the width, and there is more fringing.

With the introduction of the cage crinoline in 1856, the skirt could grow to even greater size, but fewer flounces were required to achieve the desired effect. One of the last photographs of Prince Albert, taken with Queen Victoria on March 1, 1861, shows the Queen wearing the dome-shaped cage crinoline (figure 21).

The shape of the skirt began to alter around 1860, becoming much flatter at the front and more voluminous at the back. At the same time, the neckline of the dress also changed, to include a low, square line worn over a chemisette; where the high neck was retained, a yoked effect was created by the trimming. The red satin example of about 1865 in figure 22 illustrates a practice common from the 1850s, in which two bodices were made for the same skirt, one in the high-necked day-dress style and the other with a low neck and short sleeves for evening. Another fashionable style at this date omitted the waist seam so that the bodice and skirt were made in one piece, often trimmed down the front with buttons or rosettes; occasionally a central panel of material, known as a plastron, was inserted, or two front pockets might be added.

Costumes designed specifically for use at the seaside and for walking were developing at this time (figure 25), and despite the handicap of tightly laced corsets and enormous hooped skirts, the lady of the 1860s should not be thought of as a house-bound wilting flower. A variety of different skirt-lifters were invented during this period, most of them worn like a belt inside the skirt and clipped to the inner seams to raise the long outerskirt in a series of decorative swags over the shorter underskirt (figure 23). This allowed more freedom for walking or for participating in the newly introduced game of croquet, one of the first active sports in which women could play alongside the men.

23. American walking dress, c. 1864, of blue watered silk, trimmed with black lace, white ribbon, and jet beads. Metal rings sewn into the seams are designed to be used with a skirt-lifting device to raise the skirt into swags over an underskirt. (Gift of Dorothy H. Johnston, 1940, 40.183.2)

*Godey's Lady's Book* of 1864 reported that "so much is the cavalier or looped-up style of dress in vogue, that the underskirt is now quite a consideration. As it is difficult to draw up a dress when heavily trimmed, the French modistes are now making both skirts of the same material, but the trimming, which was formerly on the outside skirt, is now applied to the short underskirt, and the outer-skirt draws up just above it, which makes a very elegant costume." Such a skirt is worn by Princess Louise in the photograph that shows her, with Queen Victoria on horseback, in 1865 (figure 24).

Archery was another popular sport for ladies, one that had been enjoyed for some time but that became particularly fashionable in the late 1860s and 1870s, as is so splendidly illustrated in the painting by William Powell Frith of his daughters, *The Fair Toxopholites* (figure 30). At the Grand National Archery Meeting in 1866 in Norwich, England, one of the prizes was a magnificent silk shawl in a presentation box (figure 26): "The shawl is one of the most elegant, rich and rare in taste Messrs. Clabburn have brought out, and the lid of the box, which is of walnut . . . had the arms of the Corporation of Norwich very effectively carved in its centre, the corner having the rose, shamrock and thistle with an inscription. . . . The gift is worthy of the occasion, and will doubtless excite interest as well as create a sharp competition among the ladies" (*The Norwich Mercury*, July 21, 1866).

Very costly shawls from India and those woven in France or in Britain at Paisley or Norwich had been a fashionable accessory since the 1830s, but as the width of the skirt grew, so the wear and manufacture of shawls reached its heyday. In December 1860 Queen Victoria wrote to her eldest daughter, Crown Princess Frederick of Prussia: "I will let you know what you can give Grandmama for Christmas, but there may not be time to get it. I know that she is passionately fond of cloaks and shawls, etc." One firm in Norwich had twenty-six styles on its books and in one year sold 32,000 shawls. The highest quality were woven in silk or in wool and could also be printed on light gauze fabrics for fashionable summer wear, but those of printed wool were only for the cheaper end of the market.

By 1866 fashion had decreed that the fullness of the skirt should be gathered up somewhat at the back, and that an overskirt should be added to the full skirt. In 1868 the great expanse of the skirt narrowed considerably at the sides, giving a much straighter silhouette in front; the fullness now moved to center back, where the primary shaping was provided by the bustle (figure 27).

**25.** Two princess-style walking or seaside costumes, c. 1865. The American dress on the left, which has a short cape and front pockets, is made of white cotton with black soutache appliqué. The English dress (right) is of raw silk trimmed with silk binding and cord buttons. (Right: Gift of Mrs. Phillip H. Gray, 1950, CI 50.105.7ab; left: Purchase, Irene Lewisohn Bequest, 1975, 1975.273)

26. Silk shawl woven by Clabburn Sons & Crisp of Norwich, England, with presentation box, awarded as a prize "for the best gold" in the ladies' section of the Grand National Archery Meeting held on July 27, 1866. (Norfolk Museums Service)

27. English day dress of chiné silk taffeta, c. 1868. The narrowing crinoline shape is accentuated by the gathered overskirt. (Purchase, Katherine Breyer Van Bomel Fund, 1980, 1980.409.1a–c)

The fashion-conscious were advised that day dresses could be subdivided into those with shorter skirts, called "walking dresses," and those with long, full skirts, suitable for flower shows or concerts, known as "afternoon costume." The aubergine walking outfit and the skating costume in the Costume Institute collection (figures 28, 29) are good illustrations of the temporary separation of costume for sport—with shorter skirts and loose-fitting jackets—from the fashionable line.

A costume without an overskirt was almost the exception after 1870. The overskirt could be separate, worn with a short bodice, or it could be part of an elongated jacket bodice; both styles were worn with an underskirt of corresponding or contrasting color. One version of this was the polonaise; described at the time as "in the Pompadour style," it was intended to be a revival of the style of the 1770s, with the overskirt hitched up and secured by buttons at the back (figure 31).

Trimmings were lavishly applied to the dress of the 1870s, and gave it much of its form and character. Dresses that had a single skirt either simulated the lines of the overskirt in the trimming or divided the skirt into two halves, the front arranged like an apron in a series of flounces, while a series of different flounces were created at the back.

**28.** English skating costume,
c. 1868, of rich maroon quilted
satin edged with white rabbit fur.
(Purchase, Friends of the Costume
Institute, 1980, 1980.72.1)

**29.** American walking dress,
c. 1870. A loose-fitting jacket is
worn with the short overskirt and
an integral underskirt of silk satin
with matching silk velvet trim.
(Gift of Mr. Frank Carrington,
1951, CI 51.26.5a–c)

30. *The Fair Toxopholites* by William Powell Frith (1819–1909), 1872. The artist has depicted his daughters engaged in the fashionable sport of archery. They are wearing overskirts gathered up only slightly at the back with the slim skirt silhouette and widening sleeve of the 1870s. (Royal Albert Memorial Museum, Exeter)

31. English day dress, early 1870s. This silk dress in the polonaise style is constructed to look like an underskirt with an open overskirt bunched up behind, in imitation of the style of the 1770s. (Purchase, Irene Lewisohn Bequest, 1986, 1986.304ab)

As the silhouette continued to narrow, the "Princess-style" dress was increasingly worn, cut all in one piece, without a waist seam, and very often with the plastron insert. From 1874 on, the front of the skirt was tied back with pairs of tapes, a technique that was developed to draw the dress more tightly around the body in front. *The Englishwoman's Magazine* of 1875 recommended "that the bodice be as long-waisted and tight-fitting as possible, the skirt as scant, and the train as full as may be."

The train had by now become essential to the fashionable dress at all times of the day, even for walking dresses, but as the bustle slipped lower and became longer, the remaining fullness of the skirt diminished, being brought together in pleats at the back to narrow the train itself.

*Myra's Journal* of 1876 sympathized with its readers: "Skirts are still so tightly strained round the body that all movement is inconvenient, and walking almost an impossibility. Bodies are made to fit like wax, with long waists and tight sleeves. . . . A woman must have a remarkably good figure to look well when dressed in this fashion; thin ones look so fragile, that one feels quite sorry for them, and stout ones generally look as if they were suffering agonies."

# Evening Dress

In general outline, the style of evening dress throughout the period between 1837 and 1877 resembled that of day dress but with an important difference—the sleeves were much shorter and the neckline was always low, "far too much so for strict delicacy to approve," warned *Ladies' Cabinet* in 1844.

In the late 1830s the neckline was off the shoulder, either straight across or "*en coeur,*" with a slight dip in the middle. The top of the bodice could be trimmed with horizontal folds of the same material or draped with a deep band of lace to form a bertha, which fell to about halfway down the sleeve. The waistline was cut low and pointed back and front, and the bodice was generally boned. By the mid-1840s, with the ever-increasing dome of the skirt, light fabrics were invariably flounced, while heavier materials were decorated with lace or trimmings (figure 32).

During the 1850s the neckline remained very low, forming a wide, shallow curve, and ribbon bows were often worn on the shoulders. Velvet bracelets and neckbands became popular as evening jewelry, and flowers, often arranged in wreaths, frequently decorated the hair. The dress itself, which acquired an increasing number of flounces, was also trimmed with flowers or with an abundance of lace and ribbons, although heavy, figured materials were left unflounced. During the visit to England in April 1855 of Napoleon III, Queen Victoria described in her diary how the Empress Eugénie dressed for dinner "in a white net dress . . . trimmed with scarlet velvet bows and bunches of white lilacs, and two bows of the same and diamond flowers in her hair."

White was worn a great deal for evening dress, and on the return visit of Victoria and Albert to Paris later in the year, the Queen wrote about another dinner: "The gentlemen in uniform, the Empress in a light, white dress with emerald and diamond diadem; and I in white with coloured ribbons (which the Emperor admired very much) and also my emeralds and diamonds, including my diadem (curious to say, we found

**32.** American evening dress, c. 1842. This red and black silk satin dress brocaded with red floral sprigs is shown with wristlets of black velvet with cut-steel buckles. (Purchase, Irene Lewisohn Bequest, 1975, 1975.128.10)

Princess Mathilde also dressed in white and with emeralds and diamonds and a diadem)."

The fashionable evening gathering depicted by Alice Walker in *Wounded Feelings* (figure 34) illustrates to perfection the profusion of lace, ribbons, and flowers used to trim the bodice and the flower-filled coiffure. Walker also includes a gentleman in dress uniform, although not quite of the rank to which Queen Victoria referred. Evening dress for those men without dress uniforms was stipulated in the 1866 *American Gentleman's Guide to Politeness and Fashion*: "The essentials of a gentleman's dress, for occasions of ceremony are a stylish well-fitting cloth coat of some dark color; nether garments to correspond, or in warm weather—white pants . . . the finest and purest linen, embroidered in white if at all. . . . A dress costume is no more complete without gloves than without boots, and to touch the pure glove of a lady with uncovered fingers is impertinent."

In the early 1860s the neckline for ladies began to include an almost square cut as well as the deep, low curve over the shoulders; at the same time the waistline became straight instead of pointed. As the full volume of the crinoline began to decrease at the top and move toward the back of the dress, the fullness, exaggerated in evening dress, became increasingly difficult to maneuver safely in an age of open fires, and there were many reports of serious accidents. As a result, such publications as *Cassell's Household Guide* issued instructions for fireproofing clothes: "Half the weight of whitening, mixed with the starch will render lace, net, muslin, gauze or any other light stuff, perfectly uninflammable. As white dresses are much worn at evening parties, where fires are often kept in grates, and numerous ladies have been burnt to death by means of their dresses catching light whilst dancing, it is hoped this receipt will not be forgotten by a lady in the habit of attending balls and parties."

The potential health hazard of evening dress was reiterated in *The Ladies' Book of Etiquette* in the late 1870s: "A light ball dress and exquisite arrangement of the hair too often make the wearer dare the inclemency of the coldest night by wearing a light shawl or hood, to prevent crushing delicate lace or flowers. Make it a fixed rule to have the head, feet and chest well protected when going to a party, even at the expense of a crushed flower or a stray curl. Many a fair head has been laid in a coffin, a victim to consumption, from rashly venturing out of a heated ball room, flushed and excited, with only a light protection against keen night air."

The author goes on to define suitable evening dress: "For small social companies, a dark silk in winter, and a pretty white muslin in summer are the most appropriate. A light head-dress of ribbon or velvet, or a plain cap, are the most suitable with this dress. For a larger party, low-necked, short-sleeved

33. French evening dress, late 1850s. This blue and white brocaded silk has a detachable bertha of white silk net, blue satin ribbon, and silk lace. It was bought in Paris by Mrs. George Gordon of Park Avenue, New York. (Gift of Mrs. Frederick van Beuren Joy, in memory of Mrs. Jacob Harsen Halsted, 1983, 1983.479.1a–c)

34. *Wounded Feelings* by Alice Walker (dates unknown), shown at the British Institution Exhibition in 1862. This painting illustrates the current taste for voluminous silk skirts, short gloves, and profusion of lace, ribbon, and flowers worn as trimmings and in the hair. The concerned companion wears an interesting short net overskirt over her blue silk dress. (The FORBES Magazine Collection, New York)

35. English evening dress, c. 1865, of red silk satin with red velvet trim, edged with ecru lace at the sleeves and neck. Figure 22 shows an alternative day bodice for this skirt. (Gift of Irene Lewisohn, 1937, 37.46.37b,c)

silk, light colored, or any of the thin goods made expressly for evening wear, with kid gloves, either of a color to match the dress or of white, black lace mittens are admissable, and flowers in the hair. A ball dress should be made of either very dressy silk, or light, thin material made over silk. It should be trimmed with lace, flowers or ribbon, and made dressy. The coiffure should be elaborate and match the dress, being either of ribbon, feather or flowers. White kid gloves, trimmed to match the dress, and white or black satin slippers, with silk stockings, must be worn."

Throughout the Victorian era gloves were essential for evening dress, but there was a range of optional accessories that could also be worn or carried. In addition to wearing flowers in the hair and on the dress, a lady might choose to carry a small bouquet, often held in an elaborate metal posy-holder. Queen Victoria, in Paris, noted that "the Empress gave me a beautiful bouquet-holder of diamonds, pearls and rubies, with the stems of enamel. She said nothing beyond hoping I would take the bouquet, and I felt shy about accepting

it, and inquired through my dresser of her dresser, who then said she hoped I would retain it. It is quite lovely." The following day she was given "a beautiful fan," another popular accessory for day and evening wear. In 1870 *Queen* magazine decreed that "no toilette can be considered complete without a fan."

By this time, the evening dress always had a train. The front of the skirt was trimmed differently from the rest, as illustrated in the Costume Institute example made by "Mon Vignon" in Paris for Mrs. Pierrepont, the wife of the American Minister to England in 1876–77 (Figure 37). The low-cut evening dress had been criticized by many as indecent throughout the period; in 1870 the novelist Charlotte Mary Yonge wrote: "Exposure is always wrong; whatever be the fashion, it is the Christian woman's duty to perceive when indecency comes in and to protest against it by her own example [and never] promote a fashion which is bad for the lower classes."

# Weddings

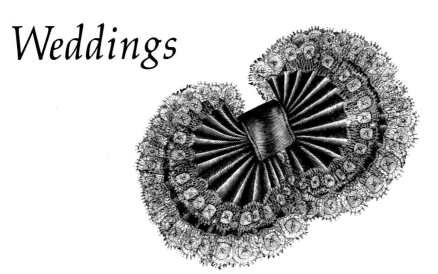

It is curious that in a period when complex rules of dress governed every occasion, the wedding dress was rather less strictly regulated. The style would have followed contemporary fashion, but the cut might be that of either day or evening dress. If the neckline was low with short sleeves, like that of evening dress, a long veil was generally worn, falling over the back of the head and secured with flowers. If the neckline was that of a day dress, with long sleeves, a flower-trimmed bonnet could be worn with a short veil. Very often, as in fashionable dress, examples survive with both types of bodice, which enabled the dress to be worn subsequently to different types of occasions.

Victoria was twenty years old and had been Queen for two years when the initial preparations for her wedding began. The likelihood of her marriage to her cousin, Prince Albert of Saxe-Coburg Gotha, had been put forward by their elders at a brief meeting several years earlier, but they had not seen each other since. On October 10, 1839, Albert and his brother visited Victoria, and five days later she proposed to him. As she later wrote, "Prince Albert could not possibly have proposed to the Queen of England. He would never have presumed to take such a liberty."

The wedding dress of creamy white Spitalfields satin was trimmed with a deep flounce of handmade Honiton lace, described as four yards long and twenty-seven inches wide. It is said that two hundred women from the village of Beer, near Honiton in Devon, were employed for eight months making the lace. The veil, sleeve ruffles, and bertha were commissioned to complete the set, and when finished, the lace designs were destroyed to prevent any possible reproduction.

The wedding itself took place on February 10, 1840 (figure 39). Albert wore the collar of the Knight of the Garter over the uniform of a Field Marshall of the British Army, and on each epaulette were large bridegroom's bows of white satin ribbon. Veils were not the exclusive prerogative of the bride;

**38.** American wedding dress, c. 1844, of ivory watered silk, with lace edging. This dress has the low neck and short sleeves typical of evening wear. (Gift of Mrs. Osborne Howes, 1950, CI 50.64.1)

Victoria's mother, the Duchess of Kent, also wore a veil, with feathers and diamonds, in the style of court dress, but other guests were instructed by Court Circular that "the exclusion of feathers is particularly desirable as they would interfere with the view of the passing scene."

White or off-white shades, following the royal example, were most popular for wedding dresses, but they were by no means the only choice, and it was quite acceptable for a fashionable bride to be married in a colored day- or evening-style gown, or even in a traveling dress, which doubled as the going-away outfit. And white was not necessarily exclusive to the bride. *Godey's Lady's Book* in 1858 depicts a bridesmaid in white silk, "distinguished from the bride by the bouquet de corsage and colored flowers for the hair."

The painting *Changing Homes* by George Elgar Hicks (figure 40) shows an exquisite bride in white who seems to have had rather young bridesmaids, judging from the three small girls

**39.** Detail from an engraving after a painting by George Hayter depicting the wedding of Queen Victoria and Prince Albert on February 10, 1840. The Queen wore a long satin train over her lace-trimmed dress, supported by twelve train bearers. Several of the senior ladies of the court wore trains and ostrich feathers, which was in keeping with court-dress regulations, but other guests were asked to omit the feathers. (Bequest of Mary Sheldon Lyon, 1947, 47.95.48)

in matching white striped dresses with pink sashes. Perhaps she was also attended by at least one young woman, as suggested by the flower-trimmed veil of her companion. The painting, shown at the Royal Academy in 1863, was well received by the *Art Journal*: "A bride in a drawing-room, surrounded by bridesmaids and a dazzling galaxy . . . affords in the bridal robes, the general gay attire and the wedding presents, favourable opportunity for the artist to display his dextrous touch."

The material used for wedding dresses also varied, and the "bridal costumes" featured in *Godey's Lady's Book* for 1861 included three dresses of white silk, one "of embroidered French muslin [a very fine cotton] with six flounces of embroidery," and a second, also of French muslin, worn with a "full wreath of leaves and orange blossoms encircling the head." A similar example in the Costume Institute collection (figure 41), lavishly trimmed with self-fabric puffings and

**40.** *Changing Homes* by George Elgar Hicks (1824–1903), shown at the Royal Academy in 1863. The bride's white satin dress has a very deep flounce of elaborate lace covering nearly the entire skirt from just below the waistline. The bride and bridesmaids hold posies, traditionally given to them after the ceremony. (The Geffrye Museum)

flutings and inset bands of white-work embroidery, was worn by a Mrs. Sullivan for her wedding at the American Legation in Paris on June 28, 1864.

Although flowers were frequently used to adorn evening dress, they were also worn in abundance with bridal outfits. Orange blossom was particularly popular during this period—Queen Victoria had worn a "wreath of orange flowers" in her hair—but it was often worn with other fresh flowers to trim the dress. By the 1870s wax orange blossom seems to have become the usual bridal flower. It was used to trim the corded silk wedding dress (figure 42) worn by Mary Taylor Gross when she married Samuel Street Smith at the Fifth Avenue Presbyterian Church on April 2, 1872. The author of *Brides and Bridals* (1872) frowned, however, on the use of this particular plant, known as one of the most fruitful of all: "Custom and romance have raised the chaplet of the orange blossoms to unmerited respect. The white of the orange flower is an impure white, and the symbolism of the plant is a reason why some other flower should be adopted."

At the wedding of the Prince of Wales to Princess Alexandra of Denmark on March 10, 1863 (figure 43), *The Illustrated London News* described the bride's dress as "white satin trimmed with chatelaines of orange-blossoms, myrtle and bouffants of tulle, with Honiton lace, the train of silver-moiré antique, trimmed with bouffants of tulle, Honiton lace, and bouquets of orange-blossom and myrtle." Lord Granville, however, in a letter to the Duchess of Manchester, thought "the dress (in my opinion, but Constance says I am wrong) was too much sunk in the Greenery—covered with too much orange flowers and green leaves."

Like his father, the Prince of Wales also married in uniform—"his mantle of the Knight of the Garter, with white ribands on each shoulder, over his uniform of the General in the Army." The wedding was held at Windsor Castle and was attended by more than nine hundred guests.

**41.** Wedding dress of very fine white cotton, known as French muslin. This elaborate costume is made up of a bodice, underskirt, and overskirt heavily trimmed with inset bands of gathered puffings and white-work embroidery. It was worn by Mrs. James Sullivan at her wedding in the American Legation in Paris on June 28, 1864. (Gift of Mrs. James Sullivan, 1926, TSR 26.250.2a–d)

**42.** American wedding dress of cream silk faille. Sprigs of artificial orange blossom decorate the bottom of the skirt. The dress was worn by Mary Taylor Gross at her wedding to Samuel Street Smith in New York in April 1872. (Gift of Louis G. Smith, in memory of his mother, Mrs. Samuel Street Smith, 1935, 35.78.1)

**43.** Photograph of the Prince and Princess of Wales on their wedding day, March 10, 1863, taken by J. J. E. Mayall. Princess Alexandra wore a profusion of orange blossoms on her lace-trimmed dress and train. See also figure 50. (Copyright reserved. Reproduced by gracious permission of Her Majesty Queen Elizabeth II)

# In Mourning

"Neglected details can lead to unhappy situations, which can cause considerable distress," the Victorian lady was warned by *Grand Maison de Noir*, and correct rules for mourning dress were suitably strict. For men the elaborate mourning of the early nineteenth century had been reduced to a black armband on the left arm, although a black crape sash and crape streamers, or "weepers," on the top hat might still be worn by the chief mourners at the funeral itself.

It was left to the women and children to demonstrate the family grief publicly. Even babies' crib sheets were sometimes embroidered with black thread. In 1860 Queen Victoria wrote to reprove her daughter, the Crown Princess of Prussia, that she had not put her five-month-old baby into mourning on the death of her husband's grandmother. "I think it quite wrong that the nursery are not in mourning. . . . You must promise me that if I should die your child or children, and those around you, should mourn; this really must be." Subsequently, the Queen described her own youngest child, Princess Beatrice, aged three, dressed in mourning for the husband of her half-sister: "Darling Beatrice looks lovely in her black silk and crape dress."

During the period of first mourning, which for a widow lasted a year and a day, the whole wardrobe was made up in black and in dull fabrics, completely covered with unrelieved matte crape. For the nine months of second mourning, she wore matte black but less crape, used in a more elaborate way as trimming. Then followed a minimum of three months of ordinary mourning, still in black but with livelier materials, such as figured silks, decorated with black lace, ribbon, or embroidery, and with jet ornamentation. The final six months of half-mourning consisted of gray, white, lavender, or violet fabrics.

In the example of first mourning illustrated here (figure 44), each panel has been completely covered with crape and edged with black bead trimming. The costume was worn by

44. French costume of silk crape for deep mourning, 1875, worn by Mrs. Mary Young Barnes of New York for both her father and her husband. (Gift of Mrs. Mary Young Barnes, 1939, 39.49.1)

Mrs. Mary Young Barnes of New York; it had been bought for her in Paris by her aunt when her father died in 1875, and she wore it again in 1878 to mourn the death of her husband.

As the rules for correct mourning wear grew ever more elaborate, authorities began to differ about the exact lengths and stages of the mourning period, but the bereaved were generally advised, on the grounds of good taste, not to make changes on the earliest permissible day. In the 1855 painting *Relenting* (figure 46) Thomas Brooks depicts a family fallen on hard times after the death of the husband, a soldier, probably killed in action in the Crimean War. Regardless of their new poverty, the young mother has dressed herself and her oldest daughter in appropriate costume. As a widow, she is in a black dress, trimmed with a white collar and cuffs, while the daughter, in shorter mourning for her father, is wearing the half-mourning shade of lavender.

The duration of mourning for ladies varied: two and a half years for a husband, eighteen months for a child, six months for a brother or sister, and six weeks for a first cousin. Since widowers, unlike widows, were permitted to remarry as soon as they liked, it was possible for a man to do so while still in mourning for his former wife. In that case *Grand Maison de Noir* advised him to leave off his armband for the wedding, but he had to wear it again the next day, and "his new wife should equally associate herself with his mourning," joining him with the appropriate level of dress, in mourning for her predecessor.

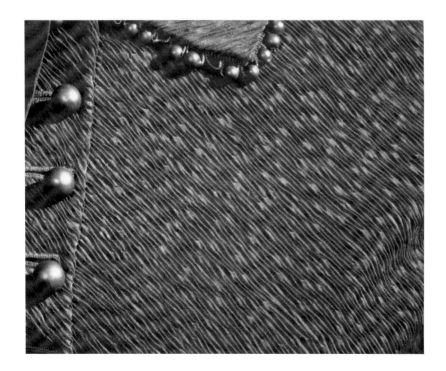

**45.** Detail of the black silk mourning crape in figure 44.

Mourning dress was not restricted to use after a death within the family. When General Mourning was declared on the death of an important national figure, the general public was asked to observe the principles of mourning dress. Court Mourning for those in the highest ranks of society was strictly observed, not only for a death in the Royal Family but also on the death of foreign royalty. On June 27, 1855, the Court Circular issued these instructions for mourning dress at court on the death of the Queen of Spain: "Ladies are to wear black dresses, white gloves, black or white shoes, feathers and fans, pearls, diamonds or plain gold or silver ornaments. The gentlemen are to wear black court dress with black swords and buckles. The Court is to change the mourning on Friday, the 12th of July. The ladies are to wear black dresses with coloured ribands, flowers, feathers and ornaments, and the gentlemen to continue the same mourning. On Friday the 19th of July next, the Court will go out of mourning." On the death of Czar Nicholas I, during the Crimean War in which England was fighting against Russia, Queen Victoria was particularly concerned that correct mourning etiquette should be observed for the unusual event of the death of a foreign monarch with whom the country was at war.

**46.** *Relenting* by Thomas Brooks (1818–1891), 1855. This painting depicts a young widow in the third stage of deep mourning; her daughter, in appropriately shorter mourning, is dressed in pale lavender, suitable for half-mourning. (Collection of Edmund J. and Suzanne McCormick)

After the death of Prince Albert at the age of forty-two from typhoid fever, the Queen was inconsolable. She withdrew from society completely, and her family and the court went into deepest mourning. The ladies attending court were instructed to wear dresses of black wool trimmed with crape, plain linen, black shoes, gloves, and crape fans. General Mourning was declared, and *The Illustrated London News* reported: "The late melancholy event which has plunged the nation in to so deep and lasting regret has, as may be imagined, created an almost incalculable demand for mourning. Never was respect paid to the memory of the great and the good more general than at the present time."

The *Englishwoman's Domestic Magazine* must have already printed its fashion plate for January 1862, including a pink and white flower-trimmed ball dress, but a postscript was added: "This ball dress might be made suitable for mourning by substituting black for the pink silk, and having a white tulle tunic spotted with black; or the dress might be composed entirely of black silk, with a black tulle tunic. In either case the flowers must, of course, be black and white, or all white." It is possible that the black watered silk evening dress in the Costume Institute collection (figure 48) was worn as General Mourning during this period.

A photograph taken by William Bambridge in March 1862 (figure 49) shows the Queen with three of her children—Princess Victoria, the Crown Princess of Prussia; Princess Alice; and Prince Alfred. All are dressed in deepest mourning. A bust of the late Prince Albert takes a prominent position; likenesses of him, mainly busts, would be included in many subsequent royal photographs. The black, crape-trimmed dress worn by Princess Beatrice, aged five, in mourning for her father, and the black woolen Highland suit of her brother Prince Arthur still survive. Black silk was permitted at court after January 1, 1862, but feathers had to be black and the mourning remained in force throughout the year. At Windsor Castle, where Albert had died, the servants were instructed to wear armbands of black crape for eight years.

In 1863, for the wedding of the Prince of Wales (figure 50), the bride and bridegroom were relieved of mourning, but the royal princesses all wore shades of half-mourning at the insistence of the Queen, who sat isolated from the rest of the congregation, still in deep mourning. She would wear mourning for Albert until her own death in 1901.

Correct accessories were required at each stage of mourning. *The Illustrated London News* in 1861 advised: "Mourning pocket handkerchiefs are frequently embroidered in black or violet, and have no trimming of lace." A large range of mourning jewelry was also available, each corresponding to the appropriate level. Jet was the most popular of these and was either left unpolished to provide a suitably dull finish or highly polished and faceted to rival the finest gemstones.

Also popular was black and white enamel set in gold and bearing suitable inscriptions, often including a central glazed panel of intricately arranged hair from the deceased. Jewelry composed completely of human hair was also fashionable mourning wear, as *Godey's Lady's Book* of 1860 explains: "Hair is at once the most delicate and lasting of our materials and survives us like Love." However, pieces of hair jewelry could be worn as love tokens, in friendship, or simply as fashionable jewelry, and in 1855, during the visit to England of Napoleon

48. English mourning dress of black watered silk for evening, c. 1861. The neck and sleeves are trimmed with lace and jet. Such a dress would have been consistent with the regulations issued for General Mourning at the death of Prince Albert. (Lent by Roy Langford)

49. Queen Victoria photographed by W. Bambridge in March 1862 with her daughter, the Crown Princess of Prussia (left), Princess Alice, and Prince Alfred, all in deepest mourning after the death of Prince Albert on December 14, 1861. (Copyright reserved. Reproduced by gracious permission of Her Majesty Queen Elizabeth II)

III and the Empress Eugénie, Queen Victoria recorded in her diary: "The Empress was touched to tears when I gave her a bracelet with my hair."

The sheer quantities of mourning, always made up in the latest fashions with its specified changes of color and material, inevitably meant a flourishing trade for the mourning departments of Victorian drapers, especially since it was considered unlucky to keep crape in the house. Some shops sold nothing but black, and one of the most fashionable and internationally prestigious of them seems to have been Jays Mourning Warehouse, which opened in Regent Street in 1841. A shoulder cape of deep mourning, worn in 1885 by the recently widowed Mrs. Ulysses S. Grant, bears a Jays of London label. In 1877 Louis Mercier wrote, in a book published by Jays: "It is by no means infrequent to meet in the first-class railway carriages on our great lines, on the quarter decks of steamers, on the Scottish rivers and lochs—even to those of the remotest Highlands, or on a return voyage in one of the magnificent steamships of the Cunard Line, the courteous and experienced employees of the House of Jay."

The dressmaking industry was notorious for low wages paid to seamstresses and for scandalous working conditions, which included overcrowding, poor ventilation, and long hours. These were exacerbated in the mourning section of the trade, where black fabric had to be worked with black thread, often in poor light. When Jays offered mourning clothes "completed with the utmost speed compatible with the requirements of taste and elegance," they often meant overnight. An inquiry, held in 1862, heard that "in a large establishment, where a great deal of mourning is made, they work from 8 or 9 until 11 p.m. all the year round." The investigators found that "mourning orders seem to be in every way especially trying; they are usually in excess of the week's work and the time allowed for their completion is too frequently very short, so that an especial sort of fatigue is added to work essentially dreary and depressing in itself."

Before the increased mechanization of the clothing industry, etiquette and rules of mourning dress had also been closely followed, but it was not proper to go into mourning until eight days after a death, on the ground that it generally took eight days to make a mourning wardrobe, and to go into mourning before that time might imply that the bereaved had vulgarly anticipated the event.

50. Engraving after a painting by William Powell Frith of the marriage of the Prince of Wales. Two of the Prince's younger brothers wore Highland outfits, as did his little nephew, the future Kaiser Wilhelm II. Queen Victoria, dressed in a black silk gown trimmed with crape, sits isolated from the congregation with her ladies-in-waiting. (The Elisha Whittelsey Collection, the Elisha Whittelsey Fund, 1949, 49.40.306)

51. American mourning dress of black silk, c. 1876. This is a day dress fashionably equipped with a bustle and train. It is trimmed with striped black satin ribbon and shown with a mourning handkerchief embroidered in white with a black printed design. (Gift of Theodore Fischer Ells, 1975, 1975.227.4)

# At Court

Victoria's court was made up of the highest levels of the international elite. In 1853, soon after his arrival in London as the new American Minister to England, James Buchanan wrote: "Society is in a most artificial position. It is almost impossible for an untitled individual who does not occupy an official position to enter the charmed circle. The richest and most influential merchants and bankers are carefully excluded." This exclusion was in fact codified; the manual *Rules and Manners of Good Society* enumerated all those eligible for presentation at court, stressing that at "trade known as retail trade the line is drawn absolutely." The importance of an individual's presentation at court was that it represented his or her official entry into this exclusive body.

Attending a court function necessitated scrupulous attention to the many rules that governed dress and behavior, rules that were frequently amended and reiterated by the Lord Chamberlain's office. These elaborately detailed regulations had developed through many years of tradition and were carefully maintained, producing a kind of protective aura around the crown.

Levees had previously served as receptions where gentlemen were presented, or introduced, to the King, while Drawing Rooms were held for the presentation of ladies and gentlemen to the King and Queen. As monarch Victoria herself held both. Application for presentation during the forthcoming season was made on January 1, by a sponsor who had already been presented. Having been presented at court thus represented a significant social distinction.

Elizabeth Bancroft, wife of the American Minister in 1847, described one such event in a letter home: "On Saturday was the dreaded Drawing-Room, on which occasion I was to be presented to the Queen. Mr. Bancroft and I left home at a quarter past one. On our arrival we passed through one or two corridors, lined by attendants with battle-axes and

52. Photograph of Queen Victoria taken by Roger Fenton after a Drawing Room held at Buckingham Palace on May 11, 1854. The Queen wears full court-dress, with a low neck, short sleeves, and a long train; in her hair are ostrich feathers and a short veil. (Copyright reserved. Reproduced by gracious permission of Her Majesty Queen Elizabeth II)

picturesque costumes . . . and were ushered into the anteroom, a large and splendid room where only the Ministers and Privy Councillors, with their families, are allowed to go with the Diplomatic Corps. . . . The room soon filled up and it was like a pleasant party, only more amusing, as the costumes of both gentlemen and ladies were so splendid. . . . At the end of this room are two doors: at the left hand everybody enters the next apartment where the Queen and her suite stand, and after going round the circle, come out at the right-hand door . . . But to go back. The left-hand door opens and Sir Edward Cust leads in the Countess Dietrichstein, who is the eldest Ambassadress, as the Countess St. Aulair is in Paris. As she enters she drops her train and the gentlemen ushers open it out like a peacock's tail. Then Madame Van de Weyer . . . then Lady Palmerston, who, as the wife of the Minister for Foreign Affairs, is to introduce the Princess Callimachi, Baroness de Beust, and myself. She stations herself by the side of the Queen and names us as we pass. . . . I was not [at] all frightened and gathered up my train with as much self-possession as if I were alone. I found it very entertaining afterward to watch the reception of the others. The Diplomatic Corps remain through the whole, the ladies standing on the left of the Queen and the gentlemen in the centre, but all others pass out immediately."

On May 11, 1854, Roger Fenton photographed Victoria and Albert after a Drawing Room held at Buckingham Palace (figure 52). She was wearing "a train of green and white brocaded silk, trimmed with white tulle and blonde, and alternate bunches of violets and pink and white may blossoms." The skirt of the dress "was of white satin, with white tulle and blonde, and bunches of violets and pink and white may blossoms to correspond with the train. Her Majesty's headdress was a wreath of violets and pink and white may blossoms and diamonds" (The Times, May 12, 1854).

Court dress for ladies at these afternoon functions was essentially that of fashionable evening dress, but what distinguished court wear was the ubiquitous white ostrich feather headdress with lace lappets or veil and the elaborate train suspended from the waist and extending up to twelve feet behind the wearer. One example, in the Costume Institute collection (figure 54), believed to date to the 1850s, is over eleven feet long and four feet wide, although at a later date two long, shaped sections of material were removed at the inner seams, causing the train to be more tapered from the ankle to the waist, to fit over a narrower skirt silhouette. The train is made from very rich cloth of silver, heavily embroidered in gold thread and flat gold strip.

White was not the only color permissible for presentation dress, but it became increasingly popular for the debutante making her first presentation. On the occasion of her marriage,

53. English court dress and train, c. 1845–50. The fabric is a silver tissue brocaded in silk floral motifs, with a deep bertha and edging of metallic lace. The costume was worn by Queen Victoria's mother, the Duchess of Kent. (Museum of London)

a society bride was usually presented again, as a member of a new family, and for this she might wear her wedding dress, suitably adapted to comply with the court requirements of short sleeves, low neck, and train.

Court dress was worn for all major court events, although exceptions were often made for royal balls or weddings, when instructions might be issued for trains or feathers to be omitted. Elizabeth Bancroft recounted some of the preparations for the State Opening of Parliament in January 1847: "This morning, when I awoke, the fog was thicker than I ever knew it, even here. . . . Mr. Bancroft's court dress had not been sent home, our servants' liveries had not made their appearance, and our carriage only arrived last night, and I had not passed judgement upon it. Fogs and tradesmen! These are the torments of London. Very soon came the tailor with embroidered dress [i.e. court-suit for Mr. Bancroft] sword and chapeau. . . . Mr. Isidore, who was to have dressed my hair at half-past ten . . . came a little before twelve, coiffure and all, which was so pretty that I quite forgave him all his sins. It was of green leaves and white fleur-de-lis, with a white ostrich feather drooping on one side. . . . My dress was black velvet with a very rich bertha. A bouquet on the front of fleur-de-lis, like the coiffure, and a Cashmere shawl, completed my array."

For men the form of court dress had been codified in the late eighteenth century, so that by the time Queen Victoria came to the throne it bore little resemblance to men's fashionable wear for day or evening The court suit comprised a silk-lined tailcoat of fine wool or velvet, knee breeches, an embroidered waistcoat of white or cream silk, silk stockings, a bicorne hat with gold-lace trim, and a sword. The coat itself was lavishly trimmed with elaborate gold embroidery, the exact width, location, and design of which were determined by the official status of the wearer.

The requirements of court dress were to present difficulties for James Buchanan, when in 1853 the American Secretary of State, Governor Marcy, issued a directive that all American ministers in Europe were to appear at their respective courts "in the simple dress of an American citizen." A potential breach of etiquette quickly became apparent, as Buchanan reported back to Marcy in an October dispatch: "Major-General Sir Edward Cust, the master of ceremonies at this court . . . expressed much opposition to my appearance at court 'in the simple dress of an American citizen.' He said I could not of course expect to be invited to court balls or court dinners, where all appeared in costumes; that her majesty never invited the bishops to balls, not deeming it compatible with their character; but she invited them to concerts, and on these occasions, as a court dress was not required, I would also be invited. He grew warm by talking and said that, whilst

54. English court train of cloth of silver, c. 1850. The edges of the train are richly embroidered by hand in gold bullion work with gold thread and flat gold strip. The train can be compared to that in the foreground of the Frith painting of the marriage of the Prince of Wales (see figure 50). The train is shown here with a dress of ivory silk that has a silk lace bertha. (Gift of Mrs. Herman A. Metz, in memory of Herman A. Metz, 1958, CI 58.69)

the queen herself would make no objections . . . yet the people of England would consider it presumption. I became somewhat indignant in my turn, and said that whilst I entertained the highest respect for her majesty . . . it would not make the slightest difference to me, individually, whether I ever appeared at court."

As the court was not in season in October, the matter remained unresolved, but Buchanan sent another dispatch in February 1854: "You will perceive by the London journals . . . that my absence from the House of Lords, at the opening of Parliament has produced quite a sensation. . . . Some time after my interview with Sir Edward Cust I determined neither to wear gold lace nor embroidery at court. It was then suggested to me that I might assume the civil dress worn by General Washington, but after examining Stewart's [sic] portrait, I observed that if I were to put on his dress and appear in it, I should render myself a subject of ridicule for life. Besides it would be considered presumption in me to affect the style of dress of the Father of his Country. It was in this unsettled state of the question, and before I had adopted any style of dress that Parliament opened."

Happily, however, by February 24 he was able to write home: "The dress question, after much difficulty, has been finally and satisfactorily settled. I appeared at the levee on Wednesday last in just such a dress as I have worn at the President's one hundred times. A black coat, white waistcoat and cravat and black pantaloons and dress-boots, with the addition of a very plain black-handled and black-hilted dress sword." He went on to explain the sword: "In the matter of my sword, I yielded without reluctance to the suggestion that a sword, at all courts of the world, is considered merely as the mark of a gentleman. I might have added that as the 'simple dress of an American citizen' is exactly that of the upper court servants, it was my purpose from the beginning to wear something which would distinguish me from them."

In 1869 the Lord Chamberlain's office issued new dress regulations for gentlemen attending court. If the court suit were of dark wool, it should have a "Dress Coat, single breasted, with straight collar, gold embroidered collar, cuffs and pocket flaps, gilt buttons" and a plain white collarless waistcoat with breeches for Drawing Rooms but trousers for Levees. The distinction between breeches and trousers was the same if the court suit were of black velvet, but the coat could have "gilt, steel or plain buttons," and the waistcoat could be black velvet or white.

Thus in 1877, when the American Minister, Edwards Pierrepont, presented his seventeen-year-old son to the Queen at a Drawing Room on May 1, the young man wore the new style of court dress in dark blue silk velvet trimmed with cut-steel buttons. A photograph of the young Mr. Pierrepont

**55.** Photograph of Mr. Edward Pierrepont wearing the blue velvet court suit in the Costume Institute collection, taken at the time of his presentation to Queen Victoria on May 1, 1877.

(figure 55) was taken at the time of his presentation, which was reported in *The Times*: "The Queen wore a dress with a train of black brocaded silk trimmed with passementerie and crape and a long white tulle veil surmounted by a coronet of sapphires and diamonds. Her Majesty also wore a necklace, brooches and earrings of sapphires and diamonds, the Riband and Star of the Order of the Garter, the Orders of Victoria and Albert, Louise of Prussia, St. Katherine of Russia, St. Isabelle of Portugal & c, and the Saxe-Coburg and Gotha Family Order. . . . The Foreign Ambassadors and Ministers, having been introduced in the order of precedence, the following presentations were made in the Diplomatic Circle . . . by the American Minister his son, Mr. Edward Pierrepont."

Presentation at court was the dream of every socially ambitious family, and in *Sidelights on English Society* (1881) the critic Grenville Murray presented a sketch of the successful debutante: "She is taken to be presented at one of the Drawing-Rooms, and if it be a novel delight it is also a trying one to find herself driving down St. James Street with bare shoulders in broad daylight. She sports a train three yards long, and a pearl necklace. On descending from their carriage in the palace yard, she and her chaperone are surrounded by young men in showy uniforms, military, naval and diplomatic, who bustle to offer their arms and murmur compliments.

"The press is so great, and the scene so imposing, that the bashful girl is glad to accept the arm of the budding diplomat, who whispers to her the names of all the great people whom they jostle. . . . The ceremony of curtseying to the Sovereign, or the Princess, cheek-by-jowl with the greatest personages in the land, endows a girl with an assurance which never forsakes her afterwards. . . . So, though her Majesty provides not so much as a cup of tea for the refreshment of her loyal subjects, who tire themselves in waiting for hours in her saloons . . . our heroine does not mind the fatigue. Her hair has got rumpled, her dress disarranged in the crush, has lost half a yard of trimming, and one of her satin shoes is slipping off; but the attaché sticks close to her, saying pleasant things, and the dragoon behind adds his word of testimony to the effect which her charms has produced. So this is to her a day of nectar-drinking. She has been presented at Court."

Throughout the first forty years of Victoria's rule, from her accession to the throne as a young girl in 1837 to the proclamations declaring her Empress in India in 1877, the fashionable ladies of England and America assiduously followed the lead set by France for them all. While the French *belles* were inclined to take fashion to its ultimate extreme, their English and American cousins were on the whole more conservative, adapting any styles that seemed too outrageous to suit their respective moral, geographical, and political climates. The highest ranking of these English-speaking ladies was undoubtedly Victoria herself, for she personified the age, both as a Queen and as a dutiful wife and mother. Although not a leader of fashion, it could be said that she led the followers and that she consciously, and conscientiously, set a royal example in dress, as in all things.

# Further Reading

Nigel Arch and Joanna Marschner, *Splendour at Court*. London: Unwin Hyman, 1987.

Elizabeth Davis Bancroft, *Letters from England*. New York: Scribners, 1904.

E. F. Benson, *Queen Victoria*. London: Chatto and Windus Ltd, 1987.

Dexter C. Bloomer, *The Life and Writing of Amelia Bloomer*. New York: Schocken Books, 1975.

Anne Buck, *Victorian Costume*. Bedford: Ruth Bean, 1984.

C. Willett Cunnington, *English Woman's Clothing in the Nineteenth Century*. London: Faber, 1937.

George Ticknor Curtis, *Life of James Buchanan*. New York: Harper and Brothers, 1883.

Frances Dimond and Roger Taylor, *Crown and Camera*. New York: Viking, 1987.

Vanda Foster, *A Visual History of Costume: The Nineteenth Century*. New York: Drama Book Publishers, 1984.

Alison Gernsheim, *Victorian and Edwardian Fashion: A Photographic Survey*. New York: Dover, 1981.

Christopher Hibbert, ed. *Queen Victoria in Her Letters and Journals*. New York: Viking, 1985.

Henry Lunettes, *The American Gentleman's Guide to Politeness and Fashion*. Philadelphia: Lippincott, 1866.

Mrs. Merrifield, *Dress as a Fine Art*. Boston: Jewett, 1854.

Ann Monsarrat, *And the Bride Wore*. London: Gentry Books, 1973.

Martha V. Pike and Janice Gray Armstrong, *A Time to Mourn*. Stony Brook, N.Y.: The Museums at Stony Brook, 1980.

Kay Staniland and Santina M. Levey, "Queen Victoria's Wedding Dress and Lace," *Costume* 17 (London) 1983.

Lou Taylor, *Mourning Dress*. London: Allen and Unwin, 1983.

Jane Tozer and Sarah Levitt, *Fabric of Society*. Powys: Laura Ashley Ltd, 1983.

Christina Walkley, *The Ghost in the Looking Glass*. London: Peter Owen, 1981.

Christina Walkley and Vanda Foster, *Crinolines and Crimping Irons*. London: Peter Owen, 1978.

Norah Waugh, *Corsets and Crinolines*. London: Batsford, 1987.